THE VENUE OF MIDNIGHT

ANUSTHA PAL

Contents

Contents

1. Fortune

Here poetess writing regarding the angels of life, Who found in your tough times, take a stand for you and help you out and turn into a fortune.

Before you,
I never knew
From how much,
I'm going through it.
Crystal world have
Stone pages,
Life gives corners and
Wedges.
I put myself distant Apart
So that,
You can't see my shallow
Parts,
This life is tough and hard.
Promise has broken under the
Canopy of woods,
I don't know how to lighten
Fire near this frosty brook.
But the raindrops come over,
my long coat
In that rain, I found you like
Fortune

And that changed everything.

2. Death Note

in this poem poetess wants to tell the story of death that exists
between
the dead body and soul. A never told breakup story of death.
I am the pieces after death,
that remain on this earth.
I can't even want to beg to
someone to make alive,
Cause my soul left me.
I wonder how close she was
to me,
I do everything according to her
what to eat, what to wear
and even what to do,
still, in this last stage, she left
me alone,
I am corpsing for my soul
to show how much I love her
and to tell her that without you
I don't want to exist and I am
decaying and lying in a crypt so
that no good fortune will ever
come to me.
yes I want to disappear in such
a way if she looks back

she isn't able to find my trace
even if she begs,
she may be, come to the graveyard to
groan on my grief
but now I am nobody.

3. Halts of brain

*Poetess brings you into the imaginary world she dreamed of in
which she is in a train with imaginary creatures.*

The halts of stations in my brain,

The train that takes me home

Is whistling in the rain

every station is the destiny of different

creatures travelling.

The miniature scenery that gave

my delight.

I m making surprised faces,

When The canopy that kneels

make me feel.

I am a journey in which you saw

dew on the leaves,

pearls in the sea and butterflies

playing in subtle greens.

and when you reach home your

life becomes a box of memories.

4. Veil

here the poetess is telling about how she used to hide from the problems every time by running from them but within the time she realises and she changed her.

I tried a lot but I fail,
I always hide in the veil
I casually walked over
The long sheet of the colour green,
I am enjoying the beauty and
Serene
Suddenly a dog bite my leg,
At that moment I feel anxious
Like a mess,
So when my mom asks,
Why do you fail?
I turn and hide in my veil.
I was riding my bicycle over
The bridge,
My brakes trot on the slope
And I hit the van and just
Pray !!
The van driver shout at me
In the frown,
Why do you fail, to put the brakes
And I breathe and I hide in my veil

One day I throw that veil
In the river of disappearance.
At that moment
Everything has changed.

5. Confusion

I am not pretty sure,
Confusion standing On my door,
I woke up and fold the Bedsheet,
I put my breakfast in my stomach and it
Knocks the door,
I became furious when I come to know
So I am hiding in the Cupboard of the room,
But time scold me and said Someone is at your door,
Go and open you are not Kid anymore!!,
I m taking feather steps and Don't make sound
When I reach the door My voice broken in the gesture
And I have a frightening face,
I take my hand over the latch of the door
Anxiety standing and hiding behind The door
I say I have another back Gate to reach,
If you don't go away
I will open it in one, two and three.
Now I pulled the hand of anxiety
and open the door,
the confusion with their Big problem
sit on the chair, Inside my brain.

then my brain speaks that, the things
that we don't know, always confuse
I will say Life is a mystery but don't confuse
Believe in your beliefs
Life is so far from what you have Imagined.
now confusion run and vanish from there.

6. Chair

Poetess have shown imaginary prose of god and their child with emphasising your attention on the chair

Every day ends with the next Surprise

You bless your smile still you hide

Everything under the chair of life.

After the long day,

God sit on the chair and

Hear whisper that you made

Your unhealed sad prose murmur

In their ear

They feel sympathetic about you,

but destiny took you to the new edge

and they try to heal you.

this universe can hear you wise

But they have something that

They bring in your life

If you see only then you can

realise, that this chair hears your sight

Otherwise, you slip just for butter

And bread life and then die.

7. Taste of time

Through this Poetess is telling about the reality that she faced. she tells about the things that she feels about when she came from dreams into reality, and what kind of facts and things she feel and put in her that make her to wrote this.

If this place is heaven,
then also we have to deal.
Betterment is a choice,
Nothing feels compulsory.
You stand over a stool of dreams,
so you feel tall,
But if you fall then you realise
That how small you are.
It is important to fall for once,
to taste the mistakes,
then life tastes bitter but better.
Wearing the same cloth for long
hit your personality,
Even the same food all the time
Makes you feel tasteless
it's like a bite of food without
Appetite.
Maybe you open your mouth
to take one bite,
When you find it tasteless

You realise,
what time does take for you
and whatever is present in front you
is the biggest surprise.

8. Clever ends

***here poetess is telling about the people with soft hearts where
every second person
want to use them for their profit, why this all happen and how is
the story written in this poem.***

My soft corners are humble
like bumble bee
I tried to be rough but that hit me
into insecurity
My coax whisper sounds that I made,
People never saw my clever ends.
I stop the hands of the clock and play
With the solitary butterflies
Frown in me turn into dew,
This quality of forgiveness make
My life.
When snakes come and hide under
My bed,
The soft corners in me feel numb
and Snakebite spread its hood.
the frission inside my head destroy
all the soft corners and end me up
on my clever ends.

9. Happiness

***In this poetess want to tell that people want to explore because they**
thought other's places are more suitable and make you feel but if you
want to find happiness everywhere.
If every day is a new life
One day I awaken and see
I am in the desert where the camel
With their hump drinking
Water from a small pond.
Then I use to realise there
Is no water but only hallucination
That kept all my wounds.
Then again I wake up into
next day into the Artist room,
Guitar and singing voice that
Sound lovely first
But the long hours of singing
Make my ear feel arrested
In a prison that wound me
In stress.
Then again I woke up
Into the hilly village
Too cool and I don't

Want to come out of
Blanket.
and I kept enjoying the
and finding that every place
is best even wherever you
are sitting is also one of the
best.

10. Wise

Some sounds are hidden in the
Home of bricks,
Some in the peace and piece
of people.
Suddenly, we have fallen into a
mental state,
our stupid tongue speaks sentences
That blow the brains.
You are just two seconds late,
but your subconscious mind knows
Something that you never gain.
Now you have few options left,
But your eyes are willing to tell the
The truth that you left in the chache.
The words that are spoken before and
after the Correct time has no meaning,
So stay cautious of your words and time.

11. Difficult Knot

here the poetess conveys the message that even in a difficult situation you have to take a stand. she is telling how situations are breaking her but still she just trying and standing with the ray of hope.

We are in the unlimited space,
One probability can take your death
The other will leave you to rest.
You push me up, but the gravity of life
pulling me down
But still, I am trying to stand with
My yellow umbrella in that crowdy
rain.
Birds with their big beak,
Try to make spots in my desolate
Dreams
But with my feathers I am
Trying to fly.

12. blackout in front of my eyes

when you are in problem everything becomes an obstacle and
small things
will hurt you.
The blackout in front of my
Eyes,
Edges that lie over the dark side.
My life brings me frock with frills,
My feeble part takes me to the crypt.
These narrow edges become
Obstacles when I run,
My limber long legs with heavy thighs
It did not support me in the blackout of
My eyes.
I must gasp some gesture to tell,
You about the train of my life,
maybe i am mythical but when you see
uneven factors in the universe maze.
then you also feel the same
I just wish god will fill the gaps that
My blackout has made.

13. Innocent guilt

being an innocent,
Is not interest anymore,
When you become a
shattered Window,
some people don't stand
near because the view is
is also shattered.
but some locks your tears
Because that want to save you
From cold winds flowing when
It snows.
Some Hashing and arranging life
For you,
Some are trying to make you
Puppet.
but still, You are making others
barren lands fertile.
You have to stop for a while.
What else needs to be escaped?
You are already hidden in the
Unknown name.
The castle that you have built is weak,
The bricks have anxiety and
The whole castle is a freak.

One day the doors of life get
Closed
Then you realise that you are
Living for foes.

14. Anguish

***The anguish behaviour is rising in people today so poetess giving
her words to this.***
Mind holding the burning coals,
You suddenly say the wrong words
And inside someone, they just flow.
You may forget what you have
Eaten,
But you are unable to forget
inopportune hurting Words
Inside your head, they are rolling
Like wheels
The tongue of adolescent
Speak and eat wounds,
so when they speak
anguish feelings speak venom
Now we need to learn from the
old times and old deeds.

15. One step ahead

***poet demonstrates through this poem that you always need to a
one step ahead of others to be the best.***

You fall some leaves from your trees,
they flow around in the serenity of the breeze.
Your leaves pigment is used by
Creatures who love to grow in green
Just wisely ink.
The letter that you have written in
the fallen leaves are in hands of the foe,
You are bending down by the planning
of beetles so that they come over on you.
beetles can't decode the
Message written on your fallen Leaves
So they take time,
And now in that time, you have to one
step forward
To prove you are ultimate and best.
otherwise, bettles come one step forward
by decoding the message,
and that's how you can save your
leaves and stems by demolishing.

16. Small things

***Poet want to tell that make your own life on your terms that only
that makes you happy at least in small things***

Cut it down

Divide in twice

The cruel world

Then even wants to split

you In thrice

Symmetry in age makes a relation

symmetric

If you change the age the unsymmetric

life may blame.

The clock and world have

endless Needs.

So first complete your beats

Supper in the evening,

Clashing and chasing windy

Night

use the divide and conquer method

and chase parts of your life

make symmetry that you love

to see in your life.

17. first or last

The first may be the last,
the last may be the first.
Clever cherishing guard
Sitting in front.
but if you are last in the
Stack so life picks you first.
your fast-changing life,
Your aspect tells about your
Mystery of creating in your time.
maybe you come last in the class
but you have created history
worldwide.
slow clumsy age of turtle and
Short panorama of butterflies
butterflies have beautiful flawless
life but end first and turtle long last
So forget the first and last,
enjoying walking moments and
left your footprints in this world
before you die.

18. Until this end

Poetess telling that you bound yourself by your own now only time can resolve this situation and before that, you have to struggle.

In the home of life
you put a lock
and everything gets off
The things that you can't
See, that may exist
is sometimes deleted by you.
Your fondness took a new Step,
But your shallowness and
Fear breaks you into tears.
I knew you again want to be
capricious mind
when you forgot every
-thing about divine,
this home holds all the data,
in the cloud to store.
but only Time has a cloud-key,
that can open that locked doors.
but until you didn't receive them
you have to feel close.

19. Beetles

In this poetess want to tell the story of small beetles and their journey

In the round flat beetles' story
In the niche of pearl drop on
green leaves.
some are brown and black,
some have a shiny glittery body,
some look like mud and some are green like leaves.
some with the dots like ladybirds
in the scenery.
There may be beetles flying
With their small wings from one
leaf to another leaf.
Crimson grey sky and the whole
Grassy village is covered by the small
Drops of rain
beetles knew that they are going to
Flow in this flood
Slowly all the world turn into a sea
For the small beetle its something
To run away with
they try to fly but one drop of rain
Is equivalent to one bucket.
they hide under the green leaf.

The maple leaf gives shade to them
And when I saw them over the leaf
It is something beautiful
But for her, it is the new edge to
Life and beetles buzzing and showing
to each other that they are alright.

20. City View

***Sometimes you don't like the city life and you get exhausted in
that
your own people only give you comfort and motivation.***

Here winds never come inside

only Stock come up and down

In a motion of to and fro

like I swing with the wings.

Cynical symphonic lights

In a parallel connection,

There is no change in the weather

Even life becomes a static

embankment,

no matter if water overflow

Sheets that are unfold

In the rooms where the doors

Are always close.

The only lights in which

I am Living is yours,

Crumble pieces that were left in

The end of the evening.

only your adorable voice

makes me wake-up and

start with a new day.

21. In my crypt

*Here poetess telling even what she thinks
about her death.*

The Rain has spattered the soil
of my grave.
I am immortal, I can manifest
About my every rave.
Absence can desire,
Presence has time to
enjoy sapphire,
Stones of my crypt spoke words
About my honesty,
Flowers over my crypt spoke how
Beautiful I was,
Time has taken my body still I am
Alive in my words and your memories.

22. Incessant Night

With marshmellow and hot
chocolate On my table,
I put all the night for search
of an incessant Night.
Days pulling my weak legs and
make Me feel paralyzed,
Nights make me nightangle
on every Single night.
Bleak head put facts like a carbon
Paper of the old days,
I don't wanna meet another day to
End this day.
Becauase here every week end
Without even asking me,
My dry throat making murmur
My death song,
If this night end there is no presence
Of me you found,
vital parts that are entirety dead
and my bad luck.

I am an incessant River of immortality,
Cause poets don't have deaths to end.
But i wish this night become a poet and
Then i will sing.

23. clingy wife

Clingy wife attached with her
Husband's lights.
Fallen in a dark submarine
Hoping for the trench in the mazy
Night.
Flower of bluebells falling
On her headspace
Turn into bell and starting
Ringing without any break,
It bleeds her ear and she fallen
On the ground
She was just started praying
for someone to save,
Her husband comes like an angel
and take her upstairs for
keeping her safe,
He erases all the thoughts of the grave,
Make her feel safe and she felt
A beautiful glorious trench in his arms
That she feels like her own space.

24. Inner voices

In this poetess talks about how our inner Voices guide us to our
destinations and try to
Give us the right directions.
Your sympathy is your
healing parts,
Points of your Dead ends,
Forgetting is a nightmare,
I am your invisible pale
Inner Voice.
Your voice texture tells
That,
I must be the frightened
part of your Inner soul.
I am mittens saving your
Hands and feeling feverish
Cold,
So, your shattered part put
me in the category of gold.
But my dead ends roars,
I make mistakes for the
Vectors of chores.
So, I kept knocking your
Door,
Until you don't look for

Someone you deserve at all.

25. don't want to Lose her

*In this poem poetess talks about how she is losing herself from her
life and she doesn't want to lose her identity anyhow and she wrote
this.*

My life is taking something from me
That I don't want to give.
The things that kept me feeling worth it.
The ocean in the eyes learned it.
How to swallow pain, because there is a lot
That I can feel but I can't spell it.
The rolling down tears from the
sliding Swing of lashes,
You breathe your sink-in soul
That put you to run for difficult goals.
I walk in flow but just stop and
Put down me like a turtle Slow,
So that I realise the crushed old
parts and just blow I am not a stone,
I m a gem that I put in my drawer.
This is Something that I don't want to
Lose.

26. Puppet

**Here the poetess trying to convey the thoughts Of someone who has been undervalued in any sort of relationship and telling the thought process*

I'm empty for you
But you are full?
How it is possible
That you make me fool,
When we are sitting on
The Front Seat together,
How do you forget to talk?
I thought the scuffle
puppets talking
From the owner's hand,
And just fallen down
Because there is no one
to watch the play.

27. Ends of the world

*Here the poetess is telling what she feels about
Ends of this world.*

Take me to the end of this
World.
I want to restart by not being a
Nerd.
My pale face knew I'm not
A star,
But I keep wishing about
My best parts.
I still keep pace to
Knew what maybe I can,
Maybe stupid or intellectual
In the bleeding bends.
I hear the story of people
Who reach the ends,
Their perception is to know
What may be the ends?
Each day I stand on the
Edge of this world and think
What should be life if this
Does the world never end?
Is the time that is ending is
everything?

Or there is something else left
To happen?
So, I keep wishing.

Thank you so much to my readers !!